THE BECOMING GAME

THE BECOMING GAME

PAULA CISEWSKI

Hanging Loose Press
Brooklyn, New York

Published by Hanging Loose Press, PO Box 150608, Brooklyn, NY 11215.

www.hangingloosepress.com

Printed in the United States of America
10 9 8 7 6 5 4 3 2 1

Hanging Loose Press thanks the New York State Council on the Arts for a grant in support of the publication of this book.

Cover Design: Roderick Brydon
Cover Photo: Celeste Nelms
Book Design: Nanako Inoue

Author Photo: Dan Michener

ISBN: 979-8-9913377-2-4

CONTENTS

ONE

TWO

THREE

FOUR

ONE

What Happened First Happened As If Nothing Was Happening.

We lived in houses someone
else built, carpooled in vehicles

named after endangered species.
What happened next was I woke

from that nightmare where I'm
everybody's dad, and the news was full

of assaulters in power
who—awake—believe they are

everybody's dads. What happens
now is language calves like a glacier.

My real family speaks in tongues.
I can't understand, and I can't

understand, but I am alive. I can't
just curl up on the ceiling

and dream. What will happen next
is that every sentence I put down

will from the ground vine
and flower: a towering future

or a flowering torture that's
any minute bound to burst wide.

My Device: An American Tangle

—After Allison Ruby's Entanglements exhibit

Waiting for the bank's drive-thru teller
to greet me from a screen I realized
I hadn't brought my cell along on errands
a little jolt of what if something happens

followed by a minor chord of disgust
something we don't yet
understand entangles us an obstacle
to our collective   to our convening

artificial mycelium cell tower fairy rings
everywhere unlike in a forest a living being
feeds the roots of trees even as it feeds on them
sounds okay from here above ground dare I say

rootless often distracted by my lack of
a pocket device with which I would at best
be doing what   devising tonight's
distraction or asking an app to direct

my lost internal sense of some people who
with theirs write whole manifestos on the light rail
and does it matter I don't know exactly where I am
when I text loved ones from my device rather than

bother them by leaving my voice on their
device is such a tidy word   devised
with an intent also difficult
to keep pushing out of my mind

that metal for mine was mined by slaves
it's so disappointing when things are
right there in the language and I live
oblivious like recently I had to visit

a museum to learn the ground bones
of buffalo strengthened colonists'
bone china cups and saucers at high tea
I have come to find working within

a net of multiple errors is an anxious
passion never not some obstacle
to repair recombine revision or
just while distracted to drop

and shatter the screen of again damn it
device vines down from Old French
devis and before that from Vulgar Latin
divisare in both cases meaning

division or to divide   my device
performed more slowly than yours
so goodbye I guess forever becomes
a true story to share with strangers

Ace of Summer

The whole world must be some forgiveness disco   I'm done
warming up   being subjected to anybody's gaze
disorganizes my features   my wander   my wounds
when anybody   stops looking at me I will   put my face back
wonder around   knowing
how it feels to be   a glamorous splat plus a little bit
the sweetest   crossing guard just wanting
to feel trusted with her orange flag   oh
strip my safety vest   I am
one flaring yes in this overmuch world

The Empress at Large

I placed a bit of seaweed on my tongue and remembered
when I was a fish. At the campfire's edge,
I misread a book's title as *The Thunder World*
and remembered what it was to storm. Having
inherited this current form from my human parents
is a fleshy pleasure. How I walk on two legs
through time. The novelty. A little cabin
by the river nobody can see is a joyful secret,
practically.   The thing about nature is
the thing. The whole thing. If you really listen,
and however long, what you hear is how
much inside the familiar you still haven't met.
When I think of my fields, I remember being
a newly planted seed. When I think of home, I remember
the beauty of not having seen one flag all week

.

The Apple Tree

This summer a tree expert came out to tell me the pockmarks
in my apples were probably maggots getting fat inside the fruit.
I judged those apples rotten, though they were perfect
for the worms, and it was perfect that I felt like a failure,

because I had failed to tend one tree. Later, a friend
came over for tea. While we looked at pictures,
something I misremembered about an image
of victory being an uneven burden worked

its way into our language. Unconsciously,
I tried to impose that on her, as if she didn't
have enough going on choosing a best path
forward. Sometimes I remember and sometimes

I misremember and all the while the president
is trying to detain everyone. I know what makes me safe-ish,
but I don't want to say it, and that's why I say it when I do
clumsily, like I just learned a new word in a second language.

Jabłka is apples in Polish, which I am teaching myself,
and which would be my other first language had it not
been smacked from my father's small mouth by a kindergarten
teacher who wanted him to assimilate whitely. What if I say

it's a gift to know what it means to have been the grower
of a maggotfeast? Can I throw the pocky apples
in the compost and learn something new before spring?

Queenie Keeps Falling Out

Even when chronically a-shuffle, even when
it's the same card landing on the floor

(there are no coincidences, or there are only
coincidences) are you still playing this game

where you pretend you have
to make a choice you have already

made? It's pleasant for a while to falter,
but plan not to live your whole life

as a coin waiting to be flipped. (Say you
won't, though the only currency of value

around here has your head on it
which makes you feel a bit lost in the dark:

half the time like a buried treasure
and the other half like a whole

undiscovered civilization.)
Sometimes a person gets

to the middle, and fortunately
or otherwise, the middle

feels like this: exactly
like the beginning, doubled.

Remember how Theseus slayed

the minotaur and saved the tributes
from the labyrinth largely because Ariadne

handed him that string but next thing
he ditched her on some island   yeah
The King of Wands is the king

of wants he's hot for everyone
it's hard to look straight at his gleaming

success teeth they're all fire
like the rest of him sincerely
able and offering to rescue us all

even if we didn't ask we believe
so hard we burn our own

problems down to please
The King who is like our cool brother
with a crown on a real natural we dare

never ask to borrow his things
a day will come he will sail

away from Us Heartbroken Saved
a little royal ourselves now glowing
in the ashes the embers of victory

Late-Capitalism Courtesy Book

If Evangeline has seven apples
but eight hangry friends who don't

like math puzzles. If sometimes
sowing a field feels like

plastering an old house as
the foundation crumbles.

To what extent are feelings
the future?

The world is/isn't
an overburdened lifeboat. Discuss.

The old orchard lay
fallow before we knew

one another in a previous
story, which was one of many

places where we earned
our educations. *Home is not*

only the place where
something is wrong

with someone. Emperor
and empathy are not, it turns

out, etymologically linked.
Emperor = empire = a big boss

who prepares us to desire
his household products. Around

the time the word empathy
was coined, Rilke sat contemplating

a panther in a cage. When
he produced that poem, what

was his faraway daughter doing?
Something is having two truth values,

which is not acceptable, says
the math professor to the lost student

in a cubicle in an office shared
by fifteen adjuncts. If I read

another freshman paper about Adolph
Hitler's vegetarianism and Nazis inventing

the VW Beetle. I don't know
if my secret prestige can

protect you if Evangeline
brings in a basket to her teacher

seven shiny red apples and
the hungry emperor's head.

At the very least, will we learn
to say *please* and *pardon me* in many

languages. Will we remember
the word for thanks at each meal.

Road Trip

—After "Road Trip" by Gary Carlson

Some groups of birds are called
a different name depending upon
which element they're in: A flock

of ducks in the sky or a paddling
of ducks on the water, for example.
Has someone forgotten to question

a traditional structure? We were,
as convention dictates, called a family
when we were near one another and

also when we were farther.
Topography
noticed occasionally

as a nice backdrop to our
ancestral spectacle-on-wheels
as we sought more suitable

terrain for what's unnamable
in each one of us. Nobody
related to this scene

has ever called any collection
of any birds a paddling.
Even on vacation, we called

what we were making *progress,*
that old saw, camper in tow. For no
other reason than to cast

our personal shadows across
plural national monuments?
Shed antler discovered at a meadow's

threshold: *Can we keep it?* Or any
small token of a world
we don't belong to? *Why don't we?*

This whole voyage is beginning
to sound autobiographical, but it's
inspired by a profound nostalgia

for nostalgia. Back inside
the bell jar of the imagination, I mean
the station wagon, moods

domino, a Rube Goldberg
contraption. We didn't know
why we were fighting. So close

for so long. Then we weren't.
Then we were again
passing a road sign

that read: PRISON
AREA DO NOT PICK
UP HITCHHIKERS.

Inside the high fence we
travel by and soon forget, lives
a group of humans often called

by different names than human.
Anybody related to this scene might
have family lost in there.

See the landscape roll by, that parched
red of memory's false heat. See the birds,
whatever they're called, borrowing the sky.

Security: An American Tangle

A little cavernous this mystery look right in the dark echoes

Held tight a treasuring impulse these queenly robes will never cover

Parse desire from nightmare two identical things but one feels like hell

Shamanic long gaze what part of the world is not home nesting with us

Border Patrol Foundation President calls tear gas totally

natural *You could literally put it on your nachos and eat it*

Same devil what a fuck shows up with fear collars for everybody

Two identical things yes one's heaven intellect alone can't guess which

This armload of not-dreaming-yet makes a great coin jangle sound when dumped

My best magic power is truth-telling rebirth it's awesome what's yours

A Philatory

—June 2017, waiting for a just verdict that did not come.

***

So much love in this
world I want to live

in it twice, let the next
moment's passing crush

my committed heart doubly.
Is that selfish?

Sorry.

***

Can't pick up right now, sorry.
Haloed by this next sorrow, sorry.

Still nostalgic for now, even
as it slips away naked.

the Internet will report this
week's sorry-ass golem lying under
oath, and so what? So sorrow.
                                                            I still need a home to
                                                                                    home to

sorrow song in
worry wrong in

***

All our hair is falling out, and so what? It gets in our art

I mean heart   same thing   the cramped space

left for this week's victim to lodge in as a memory.

Philando Castile's shot hands remember-healed, relic-nested.

***

Demonstrate   a monstrum   :   a monstrous want
Here, and here, my hope demonstration

Someone in uniform is not in jail for what one
or several witnesses caught him on video doing.

I blow my nose, sweep the floors.
The physical remains of my hope demonstration

***

Nurture, harbor, tend:
that's how the wishes grow

hallowed, misshapen, portentous:
so much more than us.

A Real Cozy Nest

Someone turned the house lights up and none of us looked great,
overstimulated and spilling all over each other.

You can light your candle off my candle, but
neither flame will burn eternal.

The baked Alaska of my anger scorched
a sticky nest of just about enough.

Wait! So she thinks you vote in gas stations??
One person at the table across from you asked the other.

Another good beginning terrifying in its future
vastness. Without our aura goggles, who to trust?

Little fruit bat observing the rat in the pantry of my anger.
Both looked pleased with how even my anger was, and how fair.

So flee to a hermitage. Night
on the mountain, campfires or fireflies,

one white horse in the distance:
her calm sends an invitation to your calm,

but not permanently. One swan: ears pricked and neck stiff:
There are the red threads again connecting even our weapons.

A little bit like playing cat's cradle:
fleeing home to try and make a real cozy nest around

my personal infinite void. A world of braided roots. A god's eye.
"Black Hole Sun" by Soundgarden stuck in a head all day.

It’s not a reference to Jesus, my anger.
My anger doing something good and private I could never

explain while the oldest tree in the forest is regarded
as just some kindling lying around.

And dollar dollar bills y’all of course flourishing
like worms in the corpse of my anger.

Ship of Fools

—After the Hieronymus Bosch painting

I think trees never die, and so never will we.
Cool cruise—are we moving? Who knows! Let's play
a game by dangling a snack from a string.
We can drink and sing and chomp at the thing.

Cool cruise—are we safe? Let's play
a game, which is a kind of prayer.
We drink and sing and chomp at the thing.
Did trees grow inside this boat or was the boat

built around trees, which are a kind of prayer?
Who knows! Those cherries look scrumptious.
Did trees grow inside the boat or was the boat
built like a wish no one remembers making?

Who knows! Those cherries were scrumptious
and aren't we content sailing away
like a wish no one remembers making?
Surely some captain or other keeps us afloat

and aren't we content sailing away?
The probably dying trees make pretty masts where wind rustles.
Surely some captain or other keeps us on course.
The fool on the bough sees clearly the bottom of his cup.

The probably dying leaves make thousands of terrible sails.
A couple fights permanently like discord is their feast
while all the fool sees clearly is the bottom of his cup.
Humans drown in the water. Birds starve in the trees.

A couple fights permanently like discord is their feast
which is a kind of a game, like thoughts and prayers, dangling
  on a string.
Humans drown in the water. Birds starve in the trees.
I think trees never die, and so never will we.

TWO

The Becoming Game, Part One

If strength need be forged in battle, I'd be sunk well before selecting any weapon. I like words. If strength need be forged in choosing them well, find me stuttering because there are so many right things to say.

Is it wrong to want a thought to have an ideal home?

Speaking of perfect homes, which seem imaginary, the artist Aki Inomata 3D-prints acrylic shells for hermit crabs to live in. They're replicas of famous architecture: for example, a miniature Bangkok skyline, or Swedish windmills.

If the shell of my greatest fear looks identical to the shell of my greatest happiness, but moldering and eternal and useless, will I still move in and hang mirrors?

Of course someone is 3D-printing a gun in his spare time, right now while I'm imagining Aki Inomata 3D-printing a tiny model of the sphinx atop a crystalline shell and a doctor 3D-printing a spleen to save a real human being.

Hermit crabs are, ironically, highly social creatures who sleep in hermit crab piles and regularly outgrow their living quarters. A cramped crab will wait near a vacant, wrong-sized shell until other poorly housed crabs join in claustrophobic anticipation for their Goldilocks to arrive: the one crab for whom the empty shelter is just right. They queue up big to small, then frenzy-swap into better fitting homes.

Most hermit crabs will not wind up sashaying along the beach with the Eiffel Tower or Taj Mahal on their backs. They might wind up living in a cracked shot glass or a scuffed-up detergent bottle cap. Some humans already live in 3D-printed homes and some humans live in trash heaps and years ago I watched a sci-fi TV series where people in warm houses 3D-printed their own 3D junk food.

I can't keep up with what we already do to ourselves.

Words are, but don't feel, entirely fabricated. Strength is forged imagining words exist to communicate a future where everybody fits or at least where everybody has some inkling of how much we need each other.

All this to say it's dizzying staying exactly here, and at least half open.

Brief Note on Forward Motion

Such terrible handwriting that
when I return to a draft I can't

tell if the speaker "wore mystery"
or "wore my story" like a cloak. Let's say

both, but let's cut "cloak," for it is an old-timey
article of clothing nobody owns. What's

pleasing about the inscrutability of the line
is that now two of something exist where

previously there was only nothing. What's
pleasing about losing the lazy image

is that now a trail is being cleared for
the speaker to move forward, cloakless,

all glow-head and breath, toward a station
for which she is ready to be ready.

Maman: An American Tangle

—with a repeated golden shovel line from Louise Bourgeois

I was at the end of a line and then I was only close to
the end, even though the baby does not unravel
a route home, which is not to say we did not travel a
predictable sticky-silk web of joy and torment
which eternally begins at the word You
said everybody wanted to leave? You must
have misunderstood my meaning. Let's begin
here and work our way there, I guess. Somewhere,

say St. Louis, a family unit parked by Louise Bourgeois' spider to
stretch legs in a sculpture park. That we were about to unravel
anything wasn't clear. The spider named *Maman* became a
looming You which we willingly stood below, a glorious torment
next to which our car was a small blue egg and we hatchlings. You
shadowlegs, You made and making vessel. You must
re-see the past or your little weavers die stunted. Say we begin
to work the brokenness of this particular somewhere,

say this country, where an actual sitting president once said to
several congresswomen *Go back where you came from*. Unravel
that. Once my mother was told a thing she didn't know was a
lie and she told me and here we are, still moving up in line, torment
or no, bearing the unspeakers' unspoken truths that web any You
to all Yous. A wedding pattern, threaded and threading. It must
be time to web some new never-ending in which we do begin
broken and work a way spoken, here somewhere.

Civil Twilight

A man who would be king hangs up his little g
reluctantly becomes a man who would be kin
a shifted syntax shifting thinking doesn't hurt
it's just embarrassing coins tumble out pockets
maybe I should lie down this contemplation cuts
we can't help but carry our hurts forward into
our eye contact as a work-around I propose
approaching this bother like an animal would
here we are living our truths making art holding
our breath while no one bothered leaving once impeached
wanting the news I'm not getting is not my gift
the value of which a stranger can't estimate

Notes toward Eternity

I leave the clever parties in a flurry to a home darkened where
I can think and be nobody standing at the foot of my shadow.

Shadows, plural: there may be more than one light
source in me casting. God I hope so all of a sudden!

I don't recall being asked to freeze or to furnish a waiting room—
a private lightbox with a lock—while the potential tarantella

in my body bruised up the bare walls. I don't recall where I first
encountered the message that Now doesn't belong to me, I only

recall knowing to avoid injury moving through time by never
grasping rails as I plummet home in love with the porch lights on:

luminous lumineers outside. What fuel. There's room for more
than one life in my life if I love more sources than borders.

"Any awareness is an increment to consciousness, an added
light," says Bachelard in *The Poetics of Reverie*. Now is still

not waiting for me. Light-headed threshold dweller, I center
and breathe. At the top cross of each breath, a fading homily.

Ace of Fall

season in which mary says my new haircut is witchy and fuck yeah

it's darker earlier darker earlier every day good morning

glitter ice cream horror movie marathon conjuring inner space

the men in power holler and cry he's the nicest person/rapist

in my annual review   the big boss wrote many corrective notes

not about a real job just general how i do on the planet

where he signed his name   the letters little animals scurrying off

i always knew i would never last in this position good morning

ready for another means of travel a truth conjured carried on

In One Thousand Years Archaeologists Uncover the Carbon Outline

You sometimes look at me through the glint of your Justice Idea
and I look at you
through the glint of mine / our backs to one another / like a couple
of aging rock

stars who are keeping the band together for the money not the
music / A slit
I was birthed through / A sharp wound with a hilt

Inside your Justice Idea, the reflection of mine inside mine inside
mine to infinity / an abstract battalion

Inside my Justice Idea, the reflection of yours inside yours inside
yours to glimpse a bardo of no

If you picture a doll or a baby picture a doll or baby
as a weapon / picture a pet sword or

never having both hands free to drink at the wedding or
to claw out the weeds / If I look at you through

The weapon of my mirror / If I stab my justice
stab my justice stab my justice into the ground / it surrounds

the property / the paint flakes off the picket fence and my friends get
so tired of helping with the repairs I must call professional help

like a fire dancer or an actual volcano to incinerate my Justice Idea
which is so upright and so sharp even as it burns / even as the ash

buries the entire county / the ash /
the ash is still falling

Poem Ending with my only Joke about Saints

On a small-hearted day, every bird sounds
like a poem I wrote ten years ago
that feels yikes now. When I shine
a light on the living end, it feels
okay. Kind of borrowed.
The glum clouds dissipate
and I get surprised to miss them.
A person's later middle years aren't
just some music piped in, making
every siphoned moment feel like
a trip to the therapist. You're entitled
to your share of the moon, even if
you're a dude. In the future, can you not
want your double edge everywhere?
On a large-hearted day, I bow to all
the talkative creatures flitting
around the bog. I know my sharp
edges make better parlor décor
than defenses. Some graffiti read,
People should do whatever the fuck they what!
So yes, I do think part of the destruction
will be incredibly positive. The Patron
Saint of Everything and The Patron
Saint of Nothing can't be
told apart. They're sick of it,
but they won't change
out of their matching robes.

Variations on Silence

Silence after traffic drone, after
a neighbor in the shared hallway
coming all hours home, after cicadas'

horny mayday reminding me—I don't
know how—of the volcanic qualities
of hope, of ash making

eventually fertile soil at someone's
current expense. After the Violent
Femmes' final encore, a ringing

in the ears that never fades but gets
forgettable. A friend's silence can be
so home-like, but then all the insects

go mute. John Cage said, of course we will
never know complete silence,
and on a somewhat related note

I have loved some people
so hard I thought surely
they could read my mind.

In a remote cabin in the woods where a writer
I know once retreated to complete her novel
in solitude, she began to hear

an unfamiliar organic squeak in the dark
and it took a long time to identify the sound
as her own eyeballs darting around

in her own terrified head. To use
silence as some umbrella term, the way
I have occasionally used poetry I just now realize,

is deeply unfair, as are some kinds
of silence, the structural kinds,
that make a cage everyone

is both inside and outside, of course
some more than others.
Why want quiet / and then / keep

asking me that question asks Joshua
Beckman in one of the books
I slipped from a shelf

in an otherwise vacant
house. Sometimes, as in
this case, the way one performs

or embodies silence is not so much
a problem of wanting
as a problem with (discipline?

privilege? distance?) matching
and variation. I'm now sure I assumed
too much too long all the while feeling

open as Rumi's reed flute. Or worse: lived
in a silence that, as Audre Lorde
cautioned, won't protect. But

the acoustics of the hollowness
amaze! What about the cozy
silence of a last standing cup when

one hesitates to leave? Whatever's
in there, even nothing, is nothing I haven't
already drunk plenty of. Anyway

this party's over. The resurrected
silence on summer evenings
after my neighbor's children have finished

singing front-porch, top-of-lungs,
about a family god is how silent?
How silent is God?

Counterglow

A star-blanked morning
can look like mourning
                                        Look again

Everything its own homonym
so sufferingly doubled right now

like to live right I have
to live twice
                                        Look again

I found a new word for
the light in the distance
that few of us can see

I shared the word with someone
so we'd have it to sing

Here comes the funny part!

1.
shouts someone's preschooler each time
Buster Keaton is about to fall,
which is almost always now.

We're in a movie house watching our hero
and his new wife construct an assemblage
of mistakes

they thought they'd live in but will
eventually abandon—spoiler alert—
strolling hand-in-hand

away down the railroad tracks. They just leave
the wreck for someone else!
The whole audience,

maybe not the preschooler,
smiles in the dark, knowing how impossible
remaining upright is.

2.
Heads or tails? The flipped coin
rolls under the effing credenza. If

the whole world is a fortune wheel, or as
Anne Lamott calls it, *forgiveness*

school, then I still resent resenting
the present situation. You can't imagine with

what vigor I have clung to my wish
for this to improve (unless

you can. Unless dizzily
dizzily you've clung, too.)

3.

Nonetheless, the card up my sleeve is
my bare wrist   a bird will
perch on   my joy is

this made thing   my life
my namesake   becoming
something else   sliding right out of the deck

4.
Getting lost on safe-ish roads
can feel like coming home. Do we know
if this is one of those roads?

5.
A caterpillar on one scale, a butterfly on the other.
which is heavier: potential or flight?

That preschooler in the movie theater said
Here comes the funny part! What does

that say? Would that hurt me? I don't
know how to talk more quieter.

Whether or not belief is relevant
All things being equal   being visible

seems like a good start

                                        I've left
                                        a light on

THREE

Ace of Winter

Season in which I discover through a small door in my cramped
house

a long-abandoned wing I've never seen, though I've lived here
some decades.

Room after room opens out palatially from one webby corridor.
Room of rusted

marching band instruments, room of easels propping up
half-finished nudes. Do I care

about spiders? Yes. Do I care about ghosts? Not sure yet. But
they'll let me stay

if I'm good. What is good? Is a ghostmind benign or viperous,
same as mine?

And they'll let me stay if I pay the ghost price. What is a
ghost price?

Blue coin in my hand, where did it come from? Where did it come

from, and, backing up a bit, when did this small door appear?

Unmentionables

When I was four years old, I slunk away from my mother in Gamble's Department Store, having been bewitched by an arrow-shaped, hand-lettered sign pointing down a staircase. It read *Lingerie*. Of course I didn't know the private delicacy of the word yet. I knew *linger* perhaps. I knew the delight of sounding out the unknown. I fit my head through the iron rails to peer down into the mystery but could see nothing. White walls. My head stuck.

Shy in public, ever wanting to remain both seen and unseen, already incapable of calling attention to a need for help, I resigned myself to what brief life there had been. *Here is my end*, I thought with a preschool-ish inner voice, much more prepared to go than feels comfortable to recall. I knelt there, lingering between existence and non, silent as a caught fawn.

After what felt like and was a very long time, one or two or probably not three quarters of an hour, my panicked mother and a store clerk located me. I suffered the indignity of the stranger manipulating my skull out of its trap as a small group of shoppers gathered around the scene.

What thread does this anecdote share with any other caught-in-between story? Just this: I did not learn what *Lingerie* meant that day, but I did not learn nothing. So many astonishing or dissatisfying answers exist for any half-formed question. And also this: one of countless experiences I walked away from different, hot-faced, having learned something accidental. Small, singular life yet intact.

Which Age of Anxiety?

Ring ring all the phone bank volunteers on antianxiety meds.
No one answers our efforts go to voicemail who leaves voicemails
ring ring.
Sky-haze reds out the sun fires wilding a thousand Canadas away.
Isn't a trip to therapy selfish California's burning too.

Don't lecture me about discipline when we don't misbehave enough.
Think of Persephone and her brave-tamed hunger save for three
damn seeds.
People need help and so few have the luxury of receiving help.
My unspecial needs my god get underground and murk things the
hell up.

What about the past turns its back stubbornly weapon drawn be
careful.
What about a dream hung by the ankles still isn't doing nothing.
Can't get lost enough but we pay our admission through the corn
maze routes.
Mother Demeter would be so proud but pride is not enough ring ring.

Ring ring our Xanax our Klonopin pomegranates we're not leaving.
We do our quests we fail our naked shadows wear us curious suits.

Notes toward my Future Nostalgia

Consider that if the old heartbreaks
demand to stay, at least their decay
feeds the root systems of us. Consider

the vacated husks of whatever
water bug a dragonfly was
until recently, ghost-clasped

to the cabin front like wee
nymph monuments.
The lapping waves glinting

sunshine: another way nature packages
light in hints, a private thing we have
inside us even when. Even when you retreat

to your cave, so to speak, which you must
luckily do, consider smallest generosities: stones
everywhere nursing the lichens and the mosses,

the eternity underfoot. Then
consider those chartreuse dragonflies
above the water like wheeeeeeee!

There is no most convenient time to erupt
from the in-between, newly winged.
Except for now, I mean.

I Asked my Students to Name an Abstract Noun —a Concept or Emotion—and the Young Man who Left his Family in Another Country Suggested from the Back Corner, "Heartbreak."

I get the future and the past confused. Nonplaces where
no one's invited to stay. I thought they were or would be home.
I will want or wanted to be home myself, not to be at home, but

to be an actual sanctuary. Instead, I am or was untenanted, held up
in the longest queue, in a winding row of strangers that becomes or
became one thing that doesn't know itself. A lot of sharp objects

everywhere. Broken glass in the garden beds. An earthworm split
in half by a shovel: will or did the two parts comfort one another?
I imagine or remember being a toddler being told all kids like

to make mudpies, being handed an empty pie tin, being told to go
have fun, but what I had when I was done was a fucking pie tin filled
with mud. Grounded on the earth, full like this of earthy memories

or wishes. The loving gazes that surround will want or wanted
us to be happy with what we create with the available materials.
And you were or will be somewhere, waiting to be home, too.

Mournifesto: An American Tangle

—after "Waterworks" by Allison Ruby

What a wall erected by people who don't know themselves
  does is kill
Our grief a closed system recycles itself in the pipe labyrinths

Not solely a function of gravity grief is/is not according
to some functional what to do with my share of the secret keening

Twenty shot dead this side's updated news outdated again again
We were just starting to feel improved to want for anything greening

Nothing exists there and not here grief sideless as if drywall
  knocked out
Who suggested we could grieve in neat sequence and put it
  behind us

Hiding grief has injured my magic imagine it's the same for you
This is my mourning your mourning our mournifesto with
  sledgehammer

The Origin of the Work of Art

"Isn't meditating on an origin dreaming?
And isn't dreaming upon an origin going beyond it?"
—Gaston Bachelard, *The Poetics of Reverie*

"...and I h^{a}d to stop there...
...almost like inserting a needle into the earth...
...I came to a conclusion that I can be
a needle woman..."
—Kimsooja

::

This is partly a story
of Kimsooja standing
straight up
like a sewing needle
pricked into
a busy street.
Kimsooja the needle
woman. She has become
insistent stillness,
stability as one
kind of lawlessness.
This is the story
of the possibilities
of degeneration.
Degenerationism,
constant. In the busy
marketplace, people
walk wide circles
around Kimsooja.

Her statement is
her rootedness.
Her rootedness is
in the way.
She is doing
a play I name
The Sorrow
of All Silent
Exclamation.

::

A belief in needle
women sends a message
about the self.

Compared to another
artist, I am
only a sometimes

needle woman.
Though I tried
standing

perfectly still
like some kind
of prick. It was

a game
of telephone.
Playing telephone

with Kimsooja's art
and the stillness
image started,

but then it circled
back meaning something
entirely different.

Let's just look at
this belief for a second
without freaking:

this is a story of wanting
to worship almost
any needle woman.

::

If I were unstill,
if I felt I needed

fastening or
six extra legs to

settle myself,
a grown woman,

then this is partly
a story about dreams,

about the day
a spider woman

crawled from
the back of a re-

curring dream
and into my ear

and laid her eggs
while I was playing

telephone with
needle woman.

::

Some women
are spiders,

not needles.
Let's feel free

to worship threads.
Any worship-object sends

a message about
the self.   Degenerationism.   Caught

webbing.   Dust,
dew, laundry pile:

all varieties of proof
beautifully

polluting
the natural world.

::

This is partly a story
of how time spiraled

away from
my girlcore.

When I woke
a grown woman

with an egg in my ear
it seemed a thousand years

between the dream-start
and a tomboy body of ten or eleven:

something happening
in the old man's basement

something hard in his trousers
my girlcore found it stupid could not

adhere meaning to it so her brain went
darkly to a corner where his webbed

name would live in secret
like a decades-long dropped call.

Isn't it crazy the only animal I ever
dream about is spiders? I wondered.

I had worshipped my weaved dreams.
His name recalled injected venom into them.

::

We can be stitch
Women,

said Needle
Woman or Spider

Woman. Who is the dreamer,
who the dream? Bless the women

who keep making openings.
Is that a threat? The dream authorities

demanded, powerless to quash
such gauzy, lawless

weaving. Inside
to outside to outside

to inside.
This is

the physical history
of reassembling a woman. How

can anyone possibly still
think human action

must be rational
to be mundane?

::

Needle Woman is a baby spider.
Spider Woman is a baby spider.
Martin Heidegger is a baby spider.
The polluters are baby spiders.
The Dream Authorities are baby spiders.
The old man's age-spotted hands are two baby spiders.
The angry cleaners are baby spiders.
The mucked up desire to worship
is a baby spider. Laughter
is a baby spider. And the old
man's mouth. If it can be named,
it is a baby spider. If it can't
be named, it is a baby spider.
Yes, I am a baby spider.
Yes, you are a baby spider.
One mustn't judge the baby spiders.
One must release the baby spiders.
They are only baby spiders.

::

Where does art even come from

A thousand years of spider dreams

I hardly understand

A thousand women threading

What saves me

::

This is the story of the day
I was reborn, and it goes
like so:
That very first day,
I already wanted to
worship someone
or something
outside, so I was
compelled to crawl
into my own ear
and lay eggs.
Baby spiders
hatched and crept
into my thinking
world. Then some
of them skittered
over into dream
world where
they grew fertile
and laid
more eggs.
The baby
spiders are
silent
exclamations,
spinning
webby corners
from my birthday
into infinity.
Since I was reborn
speaking, I stood perfectly
still and recited
my first poem. It was

this one: A Spider Poem.
The pregnant spiders'
feet were countless
needles prickling my tongue
as they scuttled
out my mouth!

Sympathy for

this devilish agony: a worn leash
whenever I recall the revelatory
solitude confettied by falling leaves
in El Parque del Buen Retiro

on the afternoon in Madrid
when I came across the Statue
of the Fallen Angel, upon
a fountain pedestal,

his tortured face gazing
up to the ideal home, away
from which he eternally
plummets. I remember aloneness,

but was not alone, having traveled
to the city with a man who bedeviled
me for years. *I can feel how much*
you want me to say I love you and that's why

I won't he said, perhaps not right
there before Lucifer, but elsewhere
                                        and often.
                                        Q: Did I love the bedeviler?

                                        A: Yes, if this is love: allowing the vortex
                                            to pull me toward his collapsed heart.
                                            I was Narcissus, enthralled. My face
                                            looked so weird.   I never did learn

                                            how not to want love, only how

not to want his. This morning I woke
from some backwater dream and blinked
away the bright decade and counting since

that Spanish fountain scene. What
a strange souvenir to keep. I never
believed I would write any love poems,
but I wrote this one, which has

revealed itself to be a belated
love poem to me. A container
for a former grief, finally,
completely released.

Notes toward Homecoming: An American Tangle

What does *lost* mean in this context? The displaced past of a less-so world?
Or when I won't write out a sentence I don't want said, groping around
in the dry of a dark spell and whoops get turned around to meet the gaze

of The Griever? O nostalgia, my half-finished manual of style.
Felt a kindness bubbling up for someone (myself) who'd belittle it, guaranteed.

"Projections change the world into the replica of one's unknown face,"
said Carl Jung. Fine, Carl Jung! The Griever's eyes are something like mine soon.
I finally wrote my unspoken sentence, looked at it, looked at it

longer, burned it, looked at it burning, smelled the overdue smoke of its
going from me, and it's gone, hushing me: a fled burrow, finally.

The Tower Fell Once

—after five pieces by Lauren Frances Evans

"...coming apart and apart like last, at pushing at,
tears for the future her job is to cry
for the future when, your job too, crying for the future
anyone anytime."
—Alice Notley, from "Travail of Nativity"

1.

A common symptom since we re-elected
        The Racist: that generalized lack

of self, that sense of missing someone
        close: your own twin you don't have.

An old trick: layer extra eyeliner and mascara
        to dissuade public tears.

Another trick: bundle our collective fears—
        an afflicted *bouquet garnis*.

Or are you your own twin: chimera,
        organs othered, birthing

unrelated needs/ideals? It's possible:
        you've read about a woman who conceived

her absorbed twin's child. Doubled or lost, you have
        no shred of medical evidence. Who needs evidence? Fear

is a human megaphone gone dumb, a structure
                of huddled limbs, going going gone numb.

2.
Erect a tower in homage to insides
matching outsides, and then a selfie

of that: an electronic reliquary:
a gulping, intestinal noooooooooooooooooooooo.

Is this the tall hole where hope
or shame shall manifest?

Both too human.
Both so compostable.

Fissures, tunnels, an impulse to binge
while happy children make sandcastles
of the crumbling foundation.

Whose kids are these??

Before it toppled, we prayed a little—a general
summons—were just putting it out there, in case.

I often
think of motherhood: The baby

I held a long tunnel ago.   My message to my child
is what I manage still to care for. I play telephone

with a future memory.
It's happening

also hurting
that feeling of being
almost home.

3.

Desire: from the Latin “de sedire” or “from the stars”

Pink is a furious color, and

muzzle-tongued, because

a sunset people has lost itself

and cindered the myth of the moon.

The want-what of us cindered it. We, the people

cindered it, having grown moon-weary but never

unfriending it, just neglecting its glow above

our occupied heads. The moon saved for us one

star-clung parable about a human who refused

to fold in on herself and become her own shadow.

Is that even true? We asked no one before

we heard night’s exit door click,

then more bright nothing.   No matter.

We reserved no room for answers.

4.

At the bottom dirt floor of the tower,

mostly buried

(Did I climb down? Am I fallen? Was I born here? Am I born?)

Here feels underground / feels inside myself.

Too human. So compostable.

Already, I want everything to be tenable.

The disc of light, for example, resembling the moon.

Already, others must be tired of hearing about the cool

things I do with my computer. Others must be

somewhere, believing something.

5.

The day I began this poem, the marker outside the grocery store
in Money, Mississippi, where Emmett Till was accused of
whistling was defiled. The vandals pulled off panels stating facts.

"Who knows what motivates people to do this?"
 said a rep from a PR firm.

Not fractals exactly, the way one body part resembles another. A lobe
 is a lobe is a lobe.
Or the way one birth. Or one murder.

This too became the day I learned
the historical marker at the site where
Till's lynched body was removed
from the Tallahatchie River has for years
been a popular target. "...being shot up with bullet holes..."
 "...multiple angles, different guns used...".

A belief is a thing. A thing cannot be made before it is imagined
deep underground / inside myself and so my body too is stuffed
with the structures that leave holes in us.

"Juxtaposed..." Says J.W. Milam about a photo he took, "Here is a
site marker for the home of...Emmett Till's murderer. It is preserved
and adorned with flowers."

The tower fell once we learned it was the structure we hated.
Toppled, I offered my ugliest self up, and hallelujah, no one tasted.

FOUR

The Becoming Game, Part Two

Is this half an origin story? The way shame called
"eminent domain!" and built its freeway through my youth?

When I was 21, I was a fool and a mother and grieved;
People were already dead, including the baby's father.

Motherhood was magic and it was arsenic; I swallowed
the seeds inside the fruit, plowed the field gone fallow: whoops,

that was my id surrounded by daddy stand-ins and shaman
wannabes.
Love wasn't a given so much as a white elephant, gifted

then yanked back. I probably got drunk about it. Careened into
the median of it. Then I was 31, a fool and a mother,

and often still I would run from the caring voices that never
held back the vast in-betweenness that merry-go-rounds

all love. I tried on the skull of a dragon. I tried
on the wig of a judge. The baby had grown

tween-like, balancing grief and dreams like edits of his own
choose-your-own-adventure tale. The end. The end. Just kidding.

In various corners of the apartment, we outgrew the need to
bury our
treasure before it was dead. Then I was 41, a fool and a mother?

Indeed. The baby was practically a grown man in the world
surrounded

by daddy stand-ins and shaman wannabes. I love the archetype

of the Fool. I love the Fool, *in theory*. To love the world you must
love yourself, and I wanted to, for him, and I did, and I do.
    Meanwhile,

the underworld circles, membranous, pressing on even the necks
of our most dear. I could never burn it down without burning
    down

everything. That's what I learned, those decades and these
decades beyond. This is the document of my efforts,

which have kindled an eternal flame of awkward glory
for a small family to warm itself near.

Time Faking Surprise When the Party Guests Jump Out and Yell, "Surprise!"

It's never not Time's birthday.

Time frosting one side of the moon with light.

Time licking light off the other side of the moon.

Time everywhere and nowhere like that jealous monotheistic god who keeps you waiting outside the funeral parlor in the rain.

The power cuts out in a storm. Fear and relief. The stove clock quits blinking at you for once.

That one kid who can't fall asleep at the slumber party? That kid's staring at the inky ceiling of Time.

Time borrowing my fogged-up glasses. The prescription's outdated.

Time dragging its best Ziggy Stardust bolt across we should be home by now.

Put a votive candle in a paper boat and set it afloat down the night river. That diminishing flicker of light is not Time.

Time picking at an iceberg lettuce wedge, such a disinterested blind date.

Time all during the rising action tying your bootlaces together.

Time flashing its prurient wombtomb at everyone while everyone makes small talk and looks at our shoes.

You say I'm in love with you to a clock, and the clock says it's 2:30. Don't let Time break your heart.

Time's drunk in its rustic she-shed while some perennials come in nicely.

Time's not a clock. Time's a gate we can't find because we've found it. We're still walking through it. Time seems like forever. It's a blizzard.

Time dreaming again of waking in the back seat of a moving car, no one at the wheel.

Time distracting itself from the enormity of itself by doom-scrolling Elon Musk news.

You think you're alone in your bed? You're not. You sleep with Time.

The past, the present, the future, the never: Time's eternal barber shop quartet.

Too many perfectly ripe strawberries for one person? That's just like Time.

Time catching itself in the mirror and shedding a tear, chronic as ever.

Most of Time's jokes are only funny to Time.

Time arrived sealed in a pink envelope you didn't open until I was gone.

Try to put Time away for an hour. What did you put away?

A weed, a seed, a need, a hunger without greed. Four of these things are not Time.

My ear to Time's chest: sound of the Milky Way thundering.

Time finally asks for help blowing the infinite candles out.

Ace of Spring

Season in which preparing to leave feels better than leaving. A sweet
ride stands prepped to haul me forward. Look at it gleam: my gold-leaf goal god
my road forward my neatly packed leaking. One fleeing charioteer
versus even one minor pothole will equal broken-down motion
plus popped hasp plus not progress but stalled blur. Oh hello my mess my mess

how it tumbles out dressing the road I'll follow back to a trippy
retrograde home. Studying my grand exit means readying to stay.

Love & Danger

The bare garden in spring always
feels like a stranger's.   Like the last

sentence in the world's only book.   My path
circles a plot I have tended each season

of my life.   Have I only dreamed
that I know how things grow?   If so,

the dreams were seeds.   If so, the seeds
were stars.   Once this plot was entirely

rubble and thirst.   Now it greens a heaven
everyone will water.   The last sentence

in one book and the first sentence in
another are two of countless rows.

We Didn't Know: An American Tangle

—for Camille Gage's Extinct Species Series, and for Camille

If you plucked a bright
body out of the night
sky

to give it a good scrubbing,
if you forgot and soaked
The North Star

until its fingers pruned: that's *Asteroxylon Mackiei*.

Sweet extinct being: we didn't know you
were gone because we didn't know
you were here. Our not knowing:

a gold record buried in storage, the magic
hour missed. Yes, the bots know
more music than we've forgotten,

but they don't know the quirk and jolt
between lyrics and breakfast, between
composing odes to elegies and elegies

to elegies and then a fleck of dust gets
under the microscope and whoops! Hello
new universe. We didn't know

what was gone because we didn't want to love even
one single cell more that we'd lose forever
whether that's how

forever works or not. So much to love is gone, and so
much to love is here, pants ripped back-flipping
through the run-on sentence of living

and the wind knocked out of us all.   How
to concede yet another extinct thing? Honestly,
I'm friends with too many

dead people on Facebook as is.
If our work is to feed the vine
that connects this life to the sky,

let's take turns being the xylem
then the phloem. Let's get lost
in the extant forest of trees

we can't name: that tall one,
that prickly one, that bent and drooping one
Rapunzeling its way out of nothing.

Asteroxylon Mackiei: a masterful painting of a photo
of a fossil trapped in chert. *That's*
as close to bringing back the dead as

we can get, she'd have said.   Then a flash
mob of released spores crashes
the understory.

Something We Protect Keeps Us Balanced Like Good Boats on the Sea

—with a golden shovel line by Dobby Gibson

Safety came to feel ornamental, like a beautiful tree you
are allergic to. We don't have to talk about belonging, but have

you too seen stars round as money and wanted to
make chariot wheels of half the sky? Why not be

able to admit one's bright canopy of want, or at least be willing?
Most people harbor a far-off vision of their full-fledged self. I wanted to

read your cards sans book, but I can't keep all the male authority figures straight. Start
signaling that as a flaw in the system, not in the self. Start with

a symbolic act re-authorizing that younger you who curated a
secret that functioned like a keel. Then, when you don't know a good ritual, guess.

Spoonbridge & Cherry by Claes Oldenburg

Water shoots out
the cherry stem and showers

the surrounding pool. A happy
sculpture in a postcard of a city

where it seems most residents
know someone who knows

someone who knows the couple
caught doing it after-hours, in

the bevel of that big spoon.
Audacity

versus
museum security.

And then? I never heard
the end. The two

were either arrested
or they fled, irreproachable,

all afterglow. Must I know?
Aren't private moments

infinitely deposited
into the safe of any single night?

One kind of honesty is choosing
whichever version feels most true

and in so doing reveal a truth about
the retellers, about me and you.

The Becoming Game, Part Three

A loon I can see calls to more loons
I can't. I dip my toe in the water.
I do not walk on the water.

I do not walk away from the shore.
Everywhere, something ecstatic
seems to be beginning, just a bright

feeling in the air I'm not sure I am
invited to. Usually I'm in a city. I mean,
usually I'm in a house in a city writing

the poems of an inside person who
frequents the insides of schools and museums,
a little pet-like it now seems to me. Where

the forest meets the shore, some mushrooms
have muscled their way up into being
part of the understory overnight.

Maybe it's not crucial you know this
about me, but when I was a kid who
couldn't sleep, I played this game called

"Becoming." Panther, egret, rhino, shrew:
I shifted my bones around, growing new
ones where necessary, sprouting feathers

or hooves, whiskers or tusks. Are there people
who don't need to know how it feels to be every
living thing? When you're a woman, people will

say things to you like “Lean in!” or “Think more
like a dude!” and it reminds me I never once
as a child in the dark attempted to “become”

a financially secure grown human being.
This luna moth caterpillar inches its way
along the path I’ll follow home. It’s fat, nearly

translucent, which means it’s ready
to crawl up in a tree and chrysalis. Exactly
the kind of small thrill I won’t usually

seek. My instinct is to take it off this beach
which I don’t. The patient water all around
and somehow the loon I could see is gone. No

loons and no hoot and no wail and no yodel
and no tremolo. They found each other, I’m
going to assume is what the silence means.

High Risk Enlightenment Store

Can you fault me for knowing I'm
as magic as you don't know you are? Not

just a patient person waiting in line for news,
mouthless as a luna moth, ever more preoccupied

than curious? Dreaming was the most acceptable
lockdown activity. It's when I didn't ask questions

like *what is protection what is food what will eat me.*
A small bird appeared in the grass of my dream yard

with its wings on backwards. Grey bird, black wings:
bewildered flit flit. After that, I knew to wake up each

morning and whisper to a stone, walk the stone secret
to the river and throw it in the sun glint. Waterbend.

Smokestack. The river did its constant work despite
humanity's progress, and then later, night drew its new blank.

Can you fault me for knowing I'm as magic as the blank
that draws you in, too?   An unquenchable fire

smoldered away inside the convenience store of my next sleep.
The neon sign above the glass door blinked HIGH RISK

ENLIGHTENMENT STORE. The sign buzzed electric, the fire
consumed the shelves and what they held. From my hiding

spot in a ditch across the street, I watched and tried to love.
What is the purpose of this life?   To be the secret

you relinquished to a stone.   What happens after death?
You watch rabbits eat green shoots in the snow.

Superfoetation

Yes, it's the season of tender buds after nothing,
but too, of a boot thwucked off in the mud, a tossed diaper
blooming in the dogwood. There's unmaking in the making
of every season. One good melt and here's the sloughed off

everything suddenly on wet display. Yeah yeah, daffodils, wren
song, sugar eggs, and getting pregnant while already
pregnant, which is a thing rabbits can do, and mice can do.
We kill our gods to watch them rise, and just now when

I doublecheck what feels made up, other animals, even
the occasional human woman can do. Creation, like destruction,
is mostly one accident on top of another, is mostly doubled
up language, blood and spittle, the incubating truth

begot in the tenuous vessel of yesterday's body. Yeah yeah,
peach blossoms,
iris blades, buds and multiple clutches
of bunnies. After winter's sterile quarantine, what
singular self wouldn't I breach for a do-over,

to once again slog through fecundity's gross mess.
There's no cruelest month. I won't ascribe to that,
and—can I get a half-hallelujah—not
every gone thing will rise again. If there's to be some new start

I can't choose to neglect how this whole rebirth thing works:
Someone
help bury my dead god parts, or at least throw them in the sea.

What Is It Like to Still Love the World?

It's like how a person might join
a cluster of people in a tight hallway,

stalled because the first to arrive
at the closed door didn't try

to open it, and each late joiner assumed
someone earlier had. The smallest small

talk shuffling discomfort. Internal worlds
on mute to suit the environment. Eventually

one person gives the knob a bored turn,
and it works, and everyone exits at once, feeling

harebrained but temporarily kind
of bonded, believing they will never

again assume a door is locked until
the next time they do. Until we do. A crowd

waiting to move into a future
that won't reduce. It's like that.

What Was Your First Concert?

My first concert was a red leaf
My first concert was waiting for a ghost in the woods
Or the tiny motor that runs your love

Once I was addicted to absence
Thief of everything green
Batting at nothing that's visible to me

My first concert was a cricket in a matchbox
A chorus of masking and unmasking
So loud you didn't have to think

A horn section swaying in sharkskin
My first concert was the treeline's
sunset impression smeared on the mirror

of the river and the current a goodbye underneath
A song from memory comes on the radio and time's
accordion squeezes in or the door slams

shut on the moment and everything goes white
I was singing along to stay alive
My first concert was a hammock swaying greenless leaves

How is it you make me want to repeat everything, everything
My first concert was seeking a second heartbeat
Unapologetic, undaunted by a missed leap

ACKNOWLEDGEMENTS

Sincere gratitude to the editors of the following publications who first published some of these poems, sometimes in slightly different versions:

32 Poems: "What Was Your First Concert?" (which was later featured on *Verse Daily)* and "Superfoetation."

Anvil Tongue: "Ship of Fools" and "Sympathy for."

The Bennington Review: "Brief Note on Forward Motion."

Columba: "The Becoming Game, Part Two."

Concision: "Notes toward my Future Nostalgia," "*Maman*: An American Tangle" and "Mournifesto: An American Tangle."

Diode: "Variations on Silence."

Dream Pop: "A Philatory."

The Glacier: "The Apple Tree."

Hanging Loose: "Which Age of Anxiety?" and "Poem Ending with my Only Joke about Saints."

The Ilanot Review: "My Device: An American Tangle" and "We Didn't Know: An American Tangle."

Jet Fuel Review: "Something We Protect Keeps Us Buoyed Like Good Boats on the Sea."

The Midway Journal: "Love and Danger."

The Laurel Review: "Remember how Theseus slayed"

Plume: "Time Faking Surprise When the Party Guests Jump Out and Yell, 'Surprise!'"

Poetry Northwest: "The Empress at Large."

Posit: "Notes toward Homecoming," and "The Becoming Game, Part Three."

Prompt: "The Tower Fell Once" first appeared as "Preserved and Adorned with Flowers."

Rewilding: *Poems for the Environment* later anthologized "The Becoming Game, Part Three."

Salt Hill Journal: "Counterglow."

Sister Arts' Ekphrasis: "Road Trip" (later anthologized in *New Poets from the Midwest)*

Sister Black Press: a limited run fine art chaplet of "Counterglow."

Superstition Review: "Notes toward Eternity."

Tammy: "Late Capitalism Courtesy Book."

the tiny: "Ace of Summer," "Ace of Fall," and "Ace of Winter."

This Spectral Evidence: Segments of "The Origin of the Work of Art."

NOTES

"My Device: An American Tangle" and "Mournifesto: An American Tangle" owe thanks to Talking Image Connection.

"Poem Ending with my only Joke about Saints" nods to the title of Deborah Keenan's book *The Saint of Everything*.

"The Tower Fell Once" includes info and italicized phrases in the final section from Harriet Sinclair's 6/26/17 newsweek.com article, "Civil Rights Marker for Emmett Till Vandalized Months after his Memorial Sign was Riddled with Bullets."

The Origin of the Work of Art is Martin Heidegger's title. The opening quotes from Kimsooja are from her Art:21/Systems interview. Visit www.kimsooja.com.

"The Becoming Game, Part Three" owes much to the BBC Earth's brief video "Crabs Trade Shells in the Strangest Way."

These poems are mostly the result of a project I took on beginning in 2017 as a coping mechanism after the 2016 election. Over a cup of tea at my dining room table, I would give a tarot reading to a person I admire, take a week or so to process and take notes, then share with them a first draft of a poem inspired by the cards, our conversation, and whatever of the world had leaked in during that time. It made space for meaningful, unmediated communication about both fear and hope—more hope, in fact, than I had expected. (If someone is still deeply engaged with a question, they still have hope.) This has been one way to listen, to trust and honor alternative ways of knowing: personal, intuitive, collaborative, mythic, mystic.

The poems are in conversation and could not have been written without LM Brimmer, Feng Sun Chen, Jeanie Chung, Monica Edwards Larson, Heidi Howell Farrah, Terrance J. Fisher, Sarah Fox, Joanna Fuhrman, Elizabeth Haugen, Su Hwang, Brett Elizabeth Jenkins, Deborah Keenan, Bethany Kestner-Whitehead, Athena Kildegaard, Michael Kleber-Diggs, Haley Lasché, Eric Lorberer, Jeanne Lutz, Rachel Moritz, Alison Morse, G.E. Patterson, Juliet Patterson, Sophia Pearl, Lucas Pingel, Katharine Rauk, Fred Schmalz, Morgan Grayce Willow, Elisabeth Workman, and the memory of my brother Michael.

"Security: An American Tangle," "Notes toward Eternity," "Ace of Fall," "Which Age of Anxiety," "Mournifesto: An American Tangle," "Notes toward Homecoming: An American Tangle," and "Ace of Spring" are written in Allen Ginsberg's American sentence — 17 syllable sentences—or sometimes in tangled versions of this haiku-inspired form.

Thank you, Joanna Fuhrman, Roderick Brydon, Christine Hamm, Elizabeth Hershon, Nanako Inoue, Dick Lourie, and everyone at Hanging Loose Press for believing in this book and bringing it into the world.

My profound and ongoing gratitude for the generosity of the poetry and art friendships and communities in which I find myself and my efforts welcomed and bettered. Thank you.

And gratitude to/for Anton. Ever Anton.